Speechless: #UneasyThoughts

By

M. Jackson

Speechless: #UneasyThoughts

ISBN-13: 978-1542801386

ISBN: 1542801389

Library of Congress Control Number: 2017915287

CreateSpace Independent Publishing Platform, North Charleston, SC

Speechless

Often misunderstood, yet extremely outspoken.

Contents

Dismay

Negligence

Disallowance

Alone

Hate

LOL

Devastated

Relationship

Fault

Anticipation

Now

Mood

Lust

Uncertain

Damn

Avenues

Disappointed

Judgement

Unique

Curves

Glass Houses

Headstrong

To those who think deeply and care just as deep.

Uneasy Thoughts

Brutally honest and point blank. Will they understand, or misinterpret my desire to release this fiery volcano, exploding way down under that fuel the fire in my tank?

Change is inevitable!

Hatred

I know nothing about you, yet choose to assume.
Can't stand the site of you, let alone be in the same
room.

Known to stay away from your kind all my life.
Was taught from a young age and passed it on to my
kids add my wife.

Don't apply here or come in my store.
Only folk with fare skin do we adore.

Go back where you came from, leave right now from
this place.
Not fully knowing self or how much you are a big
ass fuckin' disgrace.

America

We prepared food, raised kids, cleaned houses, nurtured land

and picked crops of cotton buried deep in high grass.

Sun beaten -worked like a dog, disrespected, and abused. Yet,

our queens are found mysterious and sensual, the complexity

of their creamy multi-shaded skin, never comes to pass.

Content with alienating our Goddess, subjecting our back

bones to years in a system of mass incarnation.

Preying upon our weak and youthful with addictions / easy

money. Continuing with harsh, unlawful, immoral police

brutality and intimidation.

Allowing our people to engross polluted water, live in

substandard conditions, receive poor education, be injected

with disease, while consuming tainted food that in which the

government calls nutrition.

Meanwhile, we suffer with no relief during and after natural disasters. Remedies for Cancer, HIV, Sickle Cell are withheld for pharmaceuticals to benefit, as these are hugely minority effected illnesses and conditions.

Shouting"Black Lives Matter" as we are taken down by gun fire, discrimination, condemnation, injustice and unequal opportunity. Living of color living on earth, in this free country - yet are not free, the exact story they would like us not to tell. Kneeling on one knee is a mild version of torment, where there should be unity, amends, and balance for all to have opportunity to succeed and prevail.

In office, leader of this free country we call "America", is the racist, immoral, and insensitive President Donald Trump! Attempting to "Make America Great Again" with the face of our nation being nothing more than a white supremacist, misogynistic, load of bull shit chump.

Sorry massa, we will not be oppressed, denied, mistreated or

overlooked any longer.

Those "Good old days" you continuously reference, are behind

us leaving my people much wiser, as well as stronger.

Deliberate and with disgust, sleeves pulled back, our citizens

unite hand in hand, race amongst race, nation beside nation

ready to fight.

God, please give us the strength to educate these people,

stimulate love with our heads held high, faithful and steadfast

pursuing what we know to be right.

Solid role models as Colin Kaepernick and others with the

courage to take a stand and lead what we can appreciate to no

longer to be the minority.

America has never been great, but I know we can unite and

fight for justice and equality.

Brief & Perplexed

I am Woman

I must be fed in order to nourish.

Exquisiteness

Your golden heart and gorgeous face with that bright smile add substance to my day.

My existence daughter, I would deny in trade for yours any day.

Doubt

Your resistance nourishes my reluctance and so we remain adrift.

Nope. Not at all.

I don't find it particularly moving to want to undress for someone that has no interest in my future.

Blushing

Flattered by your thoughts of me.

Pruning

Removal of the unreliable gives sustenance to the living, now watch the essence amplify.

Movement

Your daily activity is far more persuasive than your current conversation.

Expectation

*Quite different for everyone, yet relative as the mood
once disappointed.*

Trust

Words mean nothing while action speak volumes.

Possibility

The endless attempt for a greater purpose with equal ambition.

Grinning

Remembering your laugh while picturing such a beautiful smile.

Fear

Not knowing the outcome of a well calculated attempt.

Losing

Watchin' a loss

Take every chance you get to communicate, create smiles, and ask questions you are unsure of. Listen to their voice, while kissing and hugging as often as you can.

Hard to watch, yet truly a blessing. Through this difficult time, don't let them doubt your love, question your motive, nor misinterpret where you stand.

That void will never be replaced, yet remain gentle, strong, and prayer filled, remembering... This tragedy - their reward is now all in God's hands.

Okay

"She will be ok." The words that dig in my heart, while trampling my spirit.

Leaving the mouth of my step father, words completely untrue causing so much rage, I could barely stand there to hear it.

How could she think I would be ok with living my days absent from guidance and direction?

This didn't just shut the door in my face - leaving me all alone, but your grandchildren as well, all needing your love and affection.

Attempting daily to stay focused, keeping my life together, and in order.

Very difficult at times being so young without a mother or a father.

Steadfast. Strong and with contempt.

Pushing forward as best I can, ignoring the loss of energy and broken heart that left my body frail and limp.

Fighting to remember the good times, all the laughs, and special moments of my mother at her best.

Deep routed. Yearning. Burning sensation in my chest, all contributing to my lack of appetite and rest.

Pray. Pray. This advice I would hear from others, not understanding the complexity of my loss.

To think I would be ok was definitely an understatement, and completely fuckin' false.

Gone

An unbelievable ache that penetrates the reality of living every day without you.

Dismay

Negligence

Many years spent with all the care in the world. Yet, you only notice when I stop.

Disallowance

*Mind boggled... knowing your worth, yet others
dwell in uncertainty??*

Alone

Surrounded by people. Immersed in activity while holding heavy conversations, yet my mind and soul are away busy at work in search for a connection that could ignite a blaze, stimulate passion, as well as excite me.

Hate

This thing is totally your own issue. Has absolutely nothing to do with me. Find love within or work toward constructive change with the things you don't like regarding yourself.
Stop hating on me.

Lol

*Funny how people want you to fit into their world....
Yet, we are brilliant individual creatures deserving
to be passionately understood with love uniquely
twirled amongst optimism, unconditional care, and
patience.*

How does this work? Smh. Hilarious!!!

Devastated

That emptiness in my heart as you pack your things,
to move out of the place you, we call home.

Relationships

Fault

You made me face what I had been denying for quite some time.

You forced me to confront what I've known to be a crime.

Unaware you went in that night for the kill.

Expressing yourself during a rage / drunken spill.

Now deep where no one goes, the air so damn tight, mood somber, the door now ajar.

This thing has its grip in me and nowhere near, barely available and you live too fuckin far.

What? Why? I can't believe this. How?

Looking forward, enjoying the moment is all the only thing I can do for now.

Smdh. This is all your fault!

Anticipation

Exhaling to calm my pulsating heart
Nervous. Shaky. Mind in a frenzy, feelings I can't
chart
Quick chime from a text received as Xanax on a
stressful day.
Intrigued, extremely attentive, I want to have you in
every way.

Now

Strange place. Loud music. People dancing. Your hand on my leg, lips on my neck. Breast fully erect. Time to go!

Mood

Observation
Conversation
Smell of your skin
Heart of a friend
Caressing and rubbing these thighs
Light it up, take a hit - let's get high
Dazed. On cloud nine
We start to unwind
Chuckle when you laugh
Me you. Hotel - you do the math
Thoughts of love
Tight fit like a glove
Wet. Wet tongue in your kiss
Soft hands touching, I so miss
Small bites up and down my side
Yearning... craving for you to be inside
Tug. Slap. Inhale. Exhale. Climax...
Lay down. Sip on some wine. Relax.

Lust

*Remembering your lips on my shoulders, you
snatching my clothes off, straddling me in air,
pulling and smelling my hair, whispering in my ear,
grabbing my flesh, flipping me over while driving it
home.
You felt good.*

Uncertain

Not sure that we are on the same page. I apologize for trying to make sense of my feelings, while attempting to understand yours.

Damn

I let you in thinking you were drastically different, turns out while observing your reflection in the mirror, add your actions, you appear as all the others.

Avenues

Seems as if you may be unaware, yet I have more than one point of entry, in which you may explore.

Must the only way to quench your thirst, strictly be in between my legs or involve my attire straggled all throughout the floor?

Disappointed

The fool I am for thinking it was more than just sex.

Judgement

Unique

How I stand out, alone on my two feet while you fit right in as the days of the week.

Curves

Disturbed as minimal society with the glance of your hour glass absorbing their airspace.

Most men relish to touch and only imagine about the taste.

Comfortable in your own skin as you conquer the occasion.

Leaving mouths open, eyes rolled, and spilled drinks with great justification.

Glass houses

Not so much different are you than I.

Your representation and where you stand is completely based on what you would like people to believe, which we all know to be a lie.

Smiles and friendly gestures, man... smdh - such a stellar performance.

Yet, when eyes are adrift, and the spot light is away, surfaces is the real you and no one, not even a child has a chance.

Mean and offensive as the kingdom in which the devil calls home.

Your mouth reminds me of a kitchen faucet, leaving everyone's business in streets to roam.

Yet, the "Christian" you proclaim to be is diminished when you mistreat innocent people in attempt to self soothe.

The judgement, lies, and negative vibes all stumble upon extremely fuckin' rude.

Kick rocks - release your clutch, all this game, add heavy politics and that stone which you would like to cast.

If only houses where made of glass...

Pondering how long yours would actually last.

Headstrong

Defying all odds, with fear in my heart.

Failure and bad blessings lurking my shadow from the damn start.

Courageous, headstrong, baffling normality - sometimes unaware how I maintain my strength.

My past currently, nestled deep within, survival mode takes me to great lengths.

A beginning of new beginnings, unyielding until my name is high up in neon lights.

Those on my team, get on board or you are about to miss this flight.

My last thoughts - *Life has a funny way of teaching things you already know. Simply don't make the same mistake twice.*

Author's Signature

Speechless: #UneasyThoughts

A poetry book by MJ

www.theauthormj.com

You can get in touch with MJ:

Email: theauthorMJ@gmail.com

Instagram: @theauthormj

Twitter: @theauthorMJ

Facebook: @theauthormj

Contributors

Menecia Jackson - Poet

Javen Parson – Front cover illustration

Shemar Rivera – Bio author

Made in the USA
Columbia, SC
30 October 2017